Newb: A Guide to the Basics of Gaming

By Corey Hardin

$\subset\theta\alpha$

Newb: A Guide to the Basics of Gaming

Copyright © 2016 Corey Hardin

First Edition, 2016

Published in the United States of America

Published by COA Publishing

ISBN-13: 978-0692717288 (COA Publishing)

ISBN-10: 0692717285

respect to any loss or damage caused or alleged to be caused directly or indirectly by the information contained in it.

DEDICATION

You gotta start somewhere, right?

Table of Contents

INTRODUCTION

Gaming is among the most popular hobbies in the world. It is one of the most common uses of PCs today. Modern computers are capable of running sophisticated programs that make today's electronic gaming possible. The challenging and exciting single-player, head-to-head, and multiplayer games we enjoy on our PC's, console, and mobile devices are all made possible by this technology.

Gaming has become an aspect of many people's daily lives, allowing them to play during breaks and other empty periods in their schedules. Whether a person has an internet connection or not, they can play a video game. Many games do not require an internet connection at all. However, the most popular games available now are played over the internet or require a constant internet connection.

Anyone can enjoy a good video game. Most of the video game players today are young people who grew up in the electronic age, surrounded by new technologies that they take for granted for both play and everyday communication.

Gaming can be have positive and negative consequences on human behavior. Gaming addiction has become an increasing problem as games have become both more sophisticated and more accessible. Many gamers today are no longer capable of separating the world of video games from their regular lives. Some gamers respond to ordinary life frustrations with the level of viciousness found in their favorite violent video games.

The current generation is defined by their use of personal computing devices. When used to make life more convenient through interconnection and ease of communication, these devices are a boon to our future leaders. If they become simply tools for constant, sustained escapism through gaming, their utility is wasted. It is vital that people understand how to balance gaming and productivity with their devices.

Gaming has its advantages and its disadvantages. Understanding how games both help us and hinder us is vital to our future as a society.

GAMING BASICS

Gaming, in its most simple definition, is the act of playing one or more games. Gaming can be done with a PC, a console, or a mobile device. Some people who consider themselves gamers play traditional board or pen-and-paper games, but the term "gamer" has come to be associated with people who play video games, especially on a console. Many console games today are as realistic and immersive as anything imagined in the pen-and-paper role playing games of yesteryear.

Modern gaming on a PC or console is challenging, exciting, and requires gamers to use their intelligence and skill to battle other players or non-player characters controlled by the game's software. This intense mental activity appeals particularly to those who would rather use their free time working their minds rather than going out with other people. Rather than spending time outdoors or in leisure environments like bars and clubs, these people make gaming a part of their daily lives.

Gamers have a myriad of different choices when it comes to the types of games they prefer to play. Video games are produced by many major game development companies, and are carried both by stores that specialize in games and supplies for gamers and by major retailers. Video games can be purchased and shipped in physical form from online stores, and many games can be purchased and downloaded instantly to both PC's and the latest consoles.

Today's gaming consoles are produced by Nintendo, Sony, and Microsoft, and gamers often argue the merits of their favorite consoles. In addition to the console, gamers can purchase specialized controllers and peripheral devices in order to make their gaming experience more enjoyable. PC games may work with simple keyboard controls, but often the purchase of a gamepad, joystick, or other accessory will make the game easier to play.

Calling oneself a "gamer" is a badge of honor in the modern video game culture. To be a gamer means not simply to play the games, but to become a part of the society of the video game. Gamers have their own lingo and ways of interacting that may be completely foreign to non-gamers playing the games. This is particularly obvious in multiplayer online games, where those who don't understand the game or speak gamer lingo are derided as "noobs."

Gamers are often the first to point out both the positive and negative effects of gaming. Scientific studies have shown that gaming increases a person's ability to analyze situations and make connections between situations or events. Studies have also shown that people who play violent video games are more likely to be violent themselves, although there is still no certainty about which causes which. Excessive gaming can also result in social isolation and be an indicator for depression. Although gaming has its benefits, there are downsides as well.

CONSOLE GAMING

Gaming consoles play an important role in the gaming world. Consoles were created to provide a hardware package and operating system geared specifically toward the playing of video games. This contrasted with the Swiss Army Knife approach of personal computers, which come in multiple hardware configurations that are often aimed at casual users of productivity software and use operating systems intended to provide functionality for any possible use.

The internal components of gaming consoles are familiar to anyone who has poked around inside a personal computer. Gaming consoles generally use top-of-the line computer components created by major electronics manufacturers in conjunction with specialized operating systems to ensure that gamers get the best possible experience from their games. Each console manufacturer has a particular focus when it comes to the components in their systems, and the difference in the internals that the manufacturer selects shows up in the price of the console. The more cutting-edge features the manufacturer packs in, the higher the console's price.

Console gaming was first introduced to the world in 1966, but the first widely available gaming console was the Magnavox Odyssey, released in 1972. Unlike the arcade games that were popular at the time, this console system was the first to allow users to play several different video games from the same system.

Although the Odyssey was the first console gaming system, it was quickly eclipsed in popularity by the Atari

2600. The 2600 system was initially popular because it allowed users to play arcade games such as Space Invaders and Asteroids at home. When a group of Atari developers left the company and formed Activision, the Atari 2600 became the first system to have third-party developers creating games for it. Soon, other developers were making cartridges for the popular console, with the competition driving the price of games down as low as $10 and of the console itself to under $100.

The second generation of video gaming consoles was launched in 1986 with Nintendo's Famicom, released in the United States as the Nintendo Entertainment System. The NES boasted a faster processor, a better sound synthesizer, and better graphics than the aging Atari 2600 system. It was quickly challenged by game developer Sega's Sega Master System. Throughout the rest of the 1980's and 90's, each generation of new gaming consoles was released in what was dubbed the Console War between Nintendo and Sega.

In 1994, Sony entered the console war with the PlayStation. After a lukewarm initial reception, Sony released the PlayStation 2 in 2000. To date, the PS2 is the best-selling console system of all time, with more than 150 million units sold. The competition was too much for Sega, which returned to arcade game development and creating games for other console systems.

Microsoft filled the void left by Sega's departure with the Xbox in 2001. Built using off-the-shelf components, the Xbox sported a Pentium 3 processor, an NVIDIA video card, and a DVD drive provided by Philips. It was also the first console to feature an integrated hard drive, eliminating the need for external memory cards.

While most of the earliest console manufacturers such as Atari and Sega no longer produce consoles, Nintendo is still a powerhouse in the gaming industry. At the time of this writing, Nintendo's Wii U is one of the eighth-generation gaming consoles, alongside Microsoft's Xbox One and Sony's PlayStation 4.

The current generation of consoles allows users to play games on game discs or by purchasing them directly off the internet. Their game controls include control pads, joysticks, and even body-tracking, movement based controllers. These consoles reproduce high-definition sound and video, and often act as complete home media centers.

COMPUTER GAMING

Many gamers prefer to use a PC over a console. Developers often release games for both PC and a console that they have an agreement with. PC gamers can often purchase and play a collection of games that would otherwise require purchasing several different consoles.

Unlike consoles, PC's don't come with the game controllers needed to play modern games. Some game developers adapt by allowing gamers to use either keyboard controls or an external controller.

PC gamers can buy any number of peripheral accessories to make their gaming faster and better. Controllers for gamers range from highly responsive gaming keyboards and mice to gamepads and joysticks. Online gamers can buy high-definition headsets with integrated microphones for communicating with their online squad members. The accessories you will need are specific to the game and the preferences of the gamer.

When you buy a console game, all you have to do is check for your console's name on the game box. If you buy the right game, it will play on your console. PC games, however, come with lists of minimum and recommended specifications. If your computer doesn't meet the minimum specifications, you can't play the game. Unlike consoles, however, you can purchase upgrades to the central processing unit (CPU), graphics processing unit (GPU) or video card, and memory to make your computer capable of playing the game.

As your computer gets older, its components become more and more out of date. A top-of-the-line computer becomes obsolete after two years, on average. If you want to play the latest games, you'll need to upgrade.

- Hard Drive – The most basic upgrade is usually the hard drive. As we use our computers, we eventually find that they're low on storage space. Purchasing a larger internal hard drive or using an external hard drive for storing media like videos and pictures is a common solution. Internal hard drives tend to be faster than external hard drives, but external hard drives are often less expensive and have the advantage of being portable.

- Memory or RAM – The most common upgrade that affects the system's performance is on RAM memory. RAM is the short-term memory of the computer. As your video game sends commands to the CPU, the computer's "brain," it builds up a backlog of commands. This backlog is stored in memory, waiting to be processed. Persistent processes, such as the operating system and the game kernel itself, also load into memory to prevent lengthy hard drive access times. For gaming, it's always the best to load the computer with the greatest amount of memory at the highest speed the motherboard is capable of supporting.

- GPU or Video Card – The next thing you'll likely have to upgrade is the GPU. GPU's, commonly called video cards, are produced by a plethora of different manufacturers and range in price from under $50 to several hundred dollars. GPU's do the heaviest work in gaming: creating and scaling the images that you see on your screen. The top games require top hardware. When purchasing a new video card, check your PC or motherboard manual to ensure that it can support the GPU upgrade you'd like to buy.

- CPU or Processor – The CPU is the brain of the computer. Computer motherboards are built to handle a specific family of CPU's. Check your motherboard's specifications for the best CPU it is capable of running. Generally, this will not be one of the latest-model CPU's. As newer CPU's are released over time, new motherboards are developed to fill the need. After two or more years, your computer's motherboard may not be able to support a modern CPU. It may be necessary to upgrade the entire motherboard.

When you upgrade your motherboard and CPU, you will often find that your old RAM is not compatible with the new system. You may even need to buy a new GPU for the system. Although you will end up laying out a lot of cash for all of the new upgrades, your new, top of the line system will continue to run the latest games for at least another two years.

MOBILE GAMING

Before the advent of smartphones and tablets, gaming was relegated to PC's and consoles. With the current advances in high-speed, energy-conservative processors and memory, mobile gaming has become an enjoyable alternative or supplement to PC and console gaming.

Before smartphones, gamers needed to buy dedicated mobile gaming devices. The earliest handheld video games were very limited in their capacity and could usually play just one game. This all changed with the Nintendo GameBoy, a handheld gaming device with swappable game cartridges similar to the console systems of the time. Several generations of the GameBoy and its competitors have been produced throughout the years. The current generation of Nintendo's GameBoy competes against mobile phone gaming by sporting two dedicated, 3D screens and having many games that aren't playable on mobile phones or other systems.

Mobile phone-based games are often reminiscent of video games from the recent past. While console and PC gaming has become focused on first-person shooters and immersive role-playing worlds, the top mobile games are strategy and resource-building games. These games lend themselves well to the touch-based controls of modern smartphones.

While PC and console games often cost $50 or more, many mobile games are free or less than $10 to buy, although optional in-game purchases can make online games very expensive over time. Because most people today already have compatible phones and can get many free or low-cost games for them, mobile gaming can be an excellent alternative for gamers with tight budgets.

ONLINE GAMING

Today's consoles, PC's, and mobile devices all have the capability to play games that are internet-connected or played solely online. Gamers playing online games can quickly become lost in them, as the interconnected nature means that real-time opponents are always available to battle or defend against. Many online games make it impossible to attack a player while that player is online, increasing a gamer's motive to play constantly.

Many online games are free to play, but players can choose to purchase upgrades, skills, and powers to use against their opponents. When gamers become addicted to rapid power-ups in these games, they can quickly find that they've put themselves deeply into debt.

While many online games can be played freely through a web browsers, there are other video games that require gamers to pay for an online service subscription in addition to the monthly fee to their Internet Service Providers. Console web services are among the most common monthly or pay-to-play subscription services.

FREE GAMING SOFTWARE

As mentioned earlier, many excellent mobile games and online-only games are available for free, as long as you avoid in-game purchases. In addition to these games, there are groups of developers who support the idea of Free, Open-Source Software (FOSS) who develop games for fun and ask for no payment. Games made by these developers can be found by doing an internet search for FOSS games or by joining a community of FOSS gamers.

There are many pirate sources available on the internet for downloading "cracked" versions of paid video games without paying. These downloads are illegal in most countries. In addition to the legal issues, the downloads generally contain viruses, Trojan horses, and other malware that can steal your personal information and/or damage your computer. It's simply not worth it to save a few bucks by using pirate sites.

LEGITIMATE, LOW COST SOFTWARE

There are several ways to buy legitimate games for a low price. One way is to find a local gaming store. Gaming stores generally allow gamers to bring in games they are no longer playing for credit. You can often find games that are a year or two old for less than $10. Most gaming stores will offer a money-back or store-credit guarantee that the game disc will work in your system.

One of the largest current video gaming platforms for PC's is Steam. Steam's draw is multi-platform gaming. A new game with full Steam integration can play on Windows, Mac, or Linux PC's – you don't have to buy a new game for each computer, and all of your games are always available from your Steam library as soon as you log in, without hunting for a game disc. You can choose to purchase and download discounted games directly from Steam, or buy a Steam activation code from a third-party provider and then download the game from Steam. Humble Bundle is a website that sells one bundled set of games at a deep discount each month. The average complete monthly bundle costs less than $30. With a few Humble Bundle purchases, a PC gamer can quickly build an extensive Steam library without breaking the budget.

GAMING ACCESSORY BASICS

40 years ago, gaming systems came with everything you would need to play any game. From keyboard-based PC games to Atari's joystick, no extra devices were needed to play a game, nor did video gamers have a desire to buy more hardware for their games. Oh, how things have changed.

Today's gamers can choose from hundreds of different accessories, available in versions ranging from basic to pro quality. If you are a serious gamer, you can quickly spend thousands of dollars on gaming accessories for your machine.

CONSOLE GAMING ACCESSORIES

The accessories that you have available will vary based on the console that you have. There are no console-agnostic accessories – every console's accessories are made specifically for that console and the games that can be played on it.

Nintendo Wii/Wii U Accessories

Nintendo's current Wii U console is backwards compatible with all of the accessories and games for the original Wii console. There are Wii/Wii U accessories for many different games and activity packs.

- Wii Nunchuk – The nunchuk is an add-on to the main controller that adds a left-hand controlled joystick and trigger button, along with the motion detection in the basic controller. Nunchuks allow the gamer to play two-handed activity games, such as boxing, and games with a joystick-controlled Z-axis.

- Wii U Motion Plus Remote – The Motion Plus controller is an enhanced version of the original Wii's motion-detection controller that provides more accurate motion detection in all axes. It's required to play several of the Wii U's games, including the popular Wii Sports Resort and Mario vs. Sonic.

- WiiFit – The WiiFit pad is used by several exercise based games. The controller measures pressure at several points on the pad. This makes it a great controller for athletic games that measure pressure and balance, like skiing and yoga. The WiiFit game that comes packaged with the controller also includes a scale that you can use over time to measure weight loss.

- Gun controllers – Used in shooting and some combat games, gun controllers usually involve placing a Wii remote into a shell shaped like a rifle or pistol. Some gun controllers are self-contained Wii remotes complete with realistic sound and force-feedback in the gun controller. These remotes come in the shapes of several different real and imagined handguns and rifles, and can cost anywhere from $20 up to several hundred dollars for large rifles.

- Sports accessories – While you can play most games just by using the controller, some people prefer to buy accessories that reflect the games they play and make them feel more realistic. Sports accessories include tennis rackets, golf clubs, and fishing rods with inserts for your Wii remote, allowing you to play your games with a more realistic feeling than simply gripping a Wii remote.

- Style accessories – From blinged-out remote covers to decals for the console, there are plenty of accessories to adapt your Wii or Wii U console to your own personal style.

This list of accessories is by no means exhaustive. One of the reasons there are so many Wii accessories is because Nintendo made it easy to simply slide a Wii remote inside an accessory, decreasing the complexity and number of components needed to make an accessory. Some games come packaged with their own accessories that are only required for that game. Notable examples include the bases and game pieces for the Skylanders and Disney Infinities games. Other accessories may simply be custom versions of a standard accessory. Whichever way you game, the many accessories for the Wii and Wii U can make your experience more fun and entertaining.

Sony PlayStation and Microsoft Xbox Accessories

There is a wide array of accessories for both the Sony PlayStation and Microsoft Xbox consoles from the manufacturers and third party manufacturers. Serious gamers will want to make sure that the accessories they buy are top quality. Don't get tricked into buying knockoff accessories that don't work as advertised.

- Controllers – Controllers for these consoles come in both wired and wireless varieties. Wireless controllers operate on radio frequency or Bluetooth. They allow you complete freedom of movement, but require charging or battery replacement. Wired controllers need no batteries, but restrict your movement to the length of the controller cord. For greater freedom of movement with a wired controller, buy a wired controller with a long cord. In addition to the choice between wired and wireless, you can buy controllers with different button configurations that are set up for different games. Many controllers have force feedback. For the PlayStation, some controllers have a special light emitter that works with the PlayStation Camera movement control sensor. In addition to obvious physical features, it's important for a gamer to look at the controller's sensitivity. A great looking controller may have low responsiveness due to poor quality internal components.

- Motion Controllers – The PlayStation's Move controller allows you to play games that require motion control. This controller looks similar to the Wii remote, and works in the same way. Internal gyroscopes and accelerometers in the controller sense movement as you swing it around. For games that track full-body movement, you can purchase the PlayStation Camera, an accessory that uses cameras and microphones to track the gamer's movements and control the game with them. Microsoft's Xbox uses the Kinect camera device, the original full-body motion tracking controller. The

Kinect is bundled with many Xbox One systems, or it can be purchased separately.

- Headsets – If you are doing any kind of multiplayer gaming, you're going to want to use a headset. Your headset should be equipped with headphones and a microphone. You can get a simple, basic quality wired headset for $20 or less. If you are a serious gamer, you'll want something higher quality. Bluetooth wireless headsets with noise-canceling microphones and HD quality sound can cost hundreds of dollars. You'll want to pick the headset that works best for your gaming and your budget.

- Keyboards – Many games and applications for the PS4 and Xbox One have text chat features. It can be a pain to scroll through letters and numbers just to write a message. With a keyboard, gamers can type out messages just like using a computer. Some console keyboards, called text pads, are even purpose-built for gaming and allow gamers to hold the pad in their hands and text with their thumbs.

- External Hard Drives – Both the PlayStation 4 and the Xbox One have built-in internal hard drives. However, the hard drive can quickly get filled up with saved data, downloaded games, game updates, and even music and movies. When this happens, you'll want to look into an external hard drive. Many manufacturers have purpose-built "game drives" for use with gaming consoles. These range in size from 500GB up to 3TB at the time of this writing. With one downloaded game taking up to 50GB of space, it should be obvious that you're going to want as much storage space as you can get.

- Travel Cases – If you do a lot of gaming, you'll end up taking your console to a LAN party or a competition at some point. Rather than simply throwing it in the trunk of your car, you'll want your console to be well protected. Console cases come with padded compartments for your console, games, and accessories.

You can choose between soft cases and hard cases for your console. Often, theme cases will even be available, decorated with graphics from your favorite video game.

Because of the popularity of the PlayStation and Xbox systems, there are countless accessories available for these consoles. Before you buy any accessory, make sure you're getting the right quality for the price you're paying.

COMPUTER ACCESSORIES

As we discussed earlier, PC's are not generally marketed as gaming machines. Even a top-of-the-line computer system probably won't sell with the game pad you'd want for playing any first-person shooter.

- Controllers – There are countless different types of controllers available for PC gaming. Unlike console controllers, you will probably need to set up controller preferences in your game. For first-person shooters, you will want to have a game pad. Purchase a joystick if you prefer flight simulation games. For racing games, you can buy steering wheel controllers. Strategy and role-playing gamers can buy special control pads for easy access to the most important functions. If you use a mouse and keyboard, you should invest in highly responsive gaming peripherals.

- Sound systems – While not required by most games, a surround-sound audio system can make your gaming more immersive. Before buying surround-sound speakers, make sure your system's sound card can handle one.

- HD Monitors – A good video card can support multiple high-definition monitors. Many cards support the same HDMI connections used on televisions, allowing you to use an HDTV purchased at a big box retail store instead of a special HD monitor. Today's PC games can often use multiple monitors to make the game easier and more fun to play.

- Laptop Case – if you are using a gaming laptop, you should think seriously about purchasing a laptop case.

The last thing you want to have happen is for your gaming laptop to be damaged or broken while traveling to a competition. A good gaming case for your laptop will not only protect your laptop but have compartments for keeping your games, controllers, and other accessories. You can even find a laptop case that fits your own style and personality.

HOW TO GET FREE OR LOW-COST GAMING ACCESSORIES

Gaming can become very expensive when you add up the costs of games and accessories. As gaming becomes more and more popular, it seems like the market is getting flooded with low-quality accessories, while the best become increasingly out of reach for the average gamer. Unless you're independently wealthy, you'll soon wonder if there is a less expensive way to get the accessories you need for playing the best games.

Professional gamers use the best accessories. Even if you have never gamed before, once you start gaming you may find that you enjoy it enough to enter tournaments. In tournaments, you will be playing against gamers who have been playing for years. You will want the best quality accessories to compete with these gamers.

One way to get free gaming accessories is through corporate promotions. Video game companies often run promotions with new games where they give away high-quality accessories to go with the game. Often, you don't even have to purchase the game – just go to the company's website and fill out an entry form for a chance to win. Even though you aren't likely to win any specific promotion, even one or two wins will net you some great gear.

Companies also run promotions on packages of "gamer food," like chips and soda. Generally, you buy the food and get a code to enter into the website. If you already buy chips or sodas on a regular basis, switch to the brands with the game gear codes for the duration of the contest. It could net you a new gaming console, games, or accessories.

If you live near an electronics recycling facility, you can check there for free or inexpensive gear. Top gamers upgrade their gear often, and you could find high-quality accessories with nothing wrong with them other than scuffs and wear marks. Check with your local facility and see if they sell working accessories; if so, stop in at least once a week to check their inventory – you never know when you'll get lucky and score an amazing deal!

Check secondhand stores, swap meets, and yard sales. Parents will often buy excellent-quality accessories for their kids, and when the kids either stop gaming or move away, the parents will donate the games and accessories to a secondhand store or sell them at a yard sale. Since gamers aren't the ones selling these accessories and games, they often won't know the value of a particular game or accessory. You can often find great gear for just a few dollars.

Your local gaming store will also be a good source of low-cost, used accessories. If you have old games and accessories that you no longer use, you can take them in and trade for a better piece of equipment. Your trade-in value for store credit will usually be higher than cash value, because the gaming shop wants you to spend your money there instead of somewhere else. Instead of trading in a game for a game, look for good deals on high-quality accessories.

If your local game shop offers a membership, take the time to sign up for it. When you buy a game or accessory, you build point values on your membership that you can use later to get pro accessories. It may take time to build up enough points, but getting the latest piece of gear for free simply by buying games you'd buy anyway will be worth it.

It may not be easy to get free or low-cost accessories for your gaming, but it can be worth it for a gamer with a lot of time and little cash.

Corey Hardin

GAMING GENRE BASICS

In gaming, a genre is a category of games grouped by the basics of their gameplay, rather than a particular style or visual impact. The genres we'll be looking at are First-Person Shooter (FPS), Role-Playing Game (RPG), Strategy, Simulation, and Social. Each genre has its own draws for different types of gamers.

Corey Hardin

FIRST-PERSON SHOOTER BASICS

First-person shooters (FPS) are currently the most popular video game genre. First-person shooter games evolved from the early two-dimensional run-jump-shoot platform games. Flight simulator games had allowed gamers a view from the cockpit, but the ability to fight from a soldier's point of view wasn't available until 1992's PC game, Wolfenstein 3D, developed by id Software. In 1993, id followed up with the wildly successful Doom. For many gamers in the 1990's, Doom was their first taste of true first-person gaming, and they loved it.

Games in the FPS genre live up to their name; the basic goal is to shoot every bad guy in sight. Although this may sound simplistic, modern FPS games employ strategic and tactical components, making them excellent for gamers with military or police experience.

Fortunately, gamers don't all need to be soldiers in order to play FPS games. The mechanics of gunmanship are built into the games. The gamer becomes the brains behind the weaponry, moving the character to the right locations in order to make the best shots.

Studies have shown that playing FPS games increases gamers' reasoning and critical thinking skills. In order to be successful in these games, players need to be able to analyze a situation quickly and make correct decisions in an instant. Spending a lot of time thinking results in getting shot. But going in with guns blazing also results in a quick kill. Players need to be able to think fast in order to win FPS games.

First-person shooters also increase hand-eye coordination. Although gamers don't need to know how to shoot a gun to play, they have to be able to move fast and aim accurately in order to make kills. In multiplayer games, you can often tell gamers with the least FPS experience by their inability to move and shoot on the fly.

The First-person shooter genre appeals to gamers for many different reasons. There are games that simply involve running from room to room shooting everything in sight. Others require a stealth approach. Some FPS games provide an entire world for the gamer to explore, complete with puzzles to solve and missions to discover.

Succeed at FPS Games

Shooters aren't just about shooting down the bad guy. In order to become a great FPS gamer, you have to start with the goal of winning the game in mind. Whether that game is a single round of multiplayer capture-the-flag or a multi-level campaign, there are some simple strategies that can make the difference between winning the game and getting stuck in a respawn loop.

- Optimize your screen settings. Make sure your screen isn't too bright or too dark for the game you're playing. Adjust the brightness so you can see clearly without straining your eyes. How is the color balance? Gamers often prefer setting their screens to a more vivid setting than they'd use for watching TV or movies.

- Check your controller's X and Y axes. Many gamers feel more comfortable with an inverted Y-axis (pushing forward on the controller looks down, pulling back looks up). How is the controller's sensitivity? When you first start gaming, you'll probably want a low sensitivity to compensate for the large controller movements you're likely to make. As your coordination gets better, you'll increase the sensitivity.

- Make each shot count. Pulling the trigger gives away your position and invites return fire. One of the most common mistakes beginning FPS gamers make is spraying shots and hoping to hit something. Take the time to practice your aim. You'll get killed a lot at first, but you'll soon become good enough to take out every one of your enemies quickly and effectively.

- Scan your area. Beginners often see an enemy and start to line up a shot only to be hit by somebody they didn't see. Take a second to look around before getting ready to fire.

- Check the map. Most FPS games include a map that shows your area, and often where enemies are located. Rather than charging into a situation, check the map and make a quick plan of how to proceed.

Get Familiar with Your Weapons

First-Person Shooters require gamers to become familiar with a wide variety of weapons. Different weapons are required in different situations. Use the wrong weapon and you'll be lucky to make it through the level. You may have a weapon that you enjoy using the most, but sticking with that weapon in every situation is not a very good idea. You'll need to get to know the basic weapon types and when to use them.

Weapons in first-person shooters generally have the same attributes as their real-life counterparts. Although the specifics will change, the basic categories are the same throughout the majority of FPS games.

Pistol

The pistol is one of the most common weapons found in a FPS. Pistols are small, have a short effective range, and a limited shot capacity. In a close-quarters situation, however, one shot from a pistol will be more likely to kill than a shot from a rifle. FPS games often sprinkle pistols and pistol ammo liberally throughout levels, since they are inexpensive and easily carried by any baddies you might kill.

Automatic Rifle

The automatic rifle is the standby of first-person shooters. These weapons have high-capacity magazines, high rates of fire, and are accurate over a distance of up to 300 meters. Because it's so easy to go through ammo quickly with this rifle simply by holding down the trigger, it's best to learn how to make single shots rather than spraying bullets.

Submachine Gun

The SMG or Uzi style weapon can be thought of as a combination of a pistol and an automatic rifle. They have the high capacity and rate of fire of an automatic rifle, but with the shorter range of a pistol. These are less likely to show up in most games, and ammo will be more sparse than ammo for pistols or automatic rifles.

Sniper Rifle

Sniper rifles are intended for long-range shooting. Sniper rifles have a low capacity, a very slow rate of fire, and require careful aim. A good sniper can take out an enemy before being sighted, and while out of range of other weapons. If you're playing a game that has a sniper rifle, take the time to master it. It will definitely be worth the practice when you surprise your enemies with headshots at 800 meters!

Shotgun

Shotguns are devastating close-quarters weapons. Shotguns have a slow rate of fire and a very small ammo capacity, but firing one shotgun blast into a massed group can easily kill or wound several enemies. If you are an aggressive player who likes to run in with guns blazing, the shotgun is your kind of weapon.

Heavy Weapons

Heavy weapons are a class of weapons with a large capacity, high rate of fire, and serious damage capabilities. Heavy weapons are usually difficult to aim, and can slow your movement if your game mechanics are set up to account for weapon weight. However, if your game allows, heavy weapons are the best choice for use against any unarmored vehicles.

Power Weapons

Power weapons are the devastating class of weapons that destroy everything in their path. If it destroys buildings or armored vehicles, it's a power weapon. Power weapons will usually have a slow recharge/reload rate after a single fire. A good example of a power weapon is an RPG or rocket launcher.

Use Your Maps

An essential element of every first-person shooter is the map. The map serves as your guide to the level or mission in your game. When you use the map, it makes playing the game much easier. Learn how to make the best use of the map to reap the greatest benefit.

The map shows the terrain or facility layout of the current area. By checking the map, you'll always know your current location in relation to the rest of the level, your teammates, and enemies (if your game supports that).

A good map will show you not just where walls and buildings are, but help you to find the best places to take cover and escape enemy forces. By checking the map before entering an area, you might notice some barrels that would make good cover. You'd run for the barrels, hide until you heard your enemies reloading, then take them out before they could get their weapons back up.

Some games have a map that shows only areas you've already been. If you get stuck and are unable to figure out how to finish a level, check your map for doors with nothing behind them or hallways that go nowhere. The end of the level is likely in an area that you just didn't realize was there, but that you can find be looking carefully at your map.

The map is one of the things that an experienced gamer will look at first when picking up a new game. How does the map work in this game? What will it do to make winning this game easier for me? Answering those questions before you go into a gaming campaign can make the difference between a great start and an early respawn.

Practice, Practice, Practice!

Only the most experienced professional gamers can pick up a brand new game and play it at a competitive level. When you first start playing first-person shooters, it can be very intimidating, even if you've played other video games all your life. The fast pace, coordination, and concentration required by a shooter is different from every other genre. How will you ever get past that first level?

The answer is practice. No one masters a skill in an hour. Even learning the button configurations can take time. Research has suggested that it takes 100 hours to obtain a skill, 1,000 hours to be proficient at it, and 10,000 hours to master it. This may seem like a daunting number of hours when it comes to gaming, but consider the fact that the best first-person shooters released today have storylines that intend for a proficient player to play between 20 and 40 hours. It can easily take 100 hours for a new gamer to finish one good first-person shooter, and building proficiency over the course of playing through a few games will be a pleasure and not a chore.

Here are some things you should focus on as you practice your FPS gaming skills:

Accuracy

Don't just focus on getting through levels as fast as you can. The military adage goes, "One shot, one kill." Any time you fire your weapon, it should kill an enemy. Not only does this conserve ammo, but the more practiced you get at aiming your weapon, the faster you'll be able to kill enemies. Practice aiming each weapon in the game for effective kills. This will pay off when playing against other players online or in tournaments.

Tactical Awareness

Whenever you have an area to move around in, you need to know exactly what's going on in that area before you move. Sounds can be the first giveaway that enemies are in the area – grunting monsters, tittering aliens, or squawking walkie-talkies can all alert you to a dangerous situation. Even if you don't hear anything, peek around walls or obstacles before moving ahead, so you don't walk right into an ambush or take a sniper's bullet. Keep an eye on your maps as well, so you always know exactly where you are. As you practice tactical awareness skills, they'll become so second nature that you'll be able to get an idea of the scenario in less than a second.

Choosing and Upgrading Weapons

In many first-person shooters, just learning which shortcut button switches to which weapon can take time. Get to know the weapon mechanics of your game. Learn which weapon is the best for which situation. When you discover a new weapon, don't barge ahead to the next challenge. Take a moment to analyze the weapon, and try it out if you are in a safe area and have enough ammo for it. If your game allows you to select and purchase weapons upgrades, take some time upgrading different weapons to see what the upgrades will do. Sometimes, you may find that completing a level requires an upgrade on a weapon that you've ignored.

Remember, first-person shooters aren't just about blasting everything that moves. They combine skill, dexterity, and strategy. Practicing the right skills will take you from being a person who plays video games to being a true gamer.

Pick a Game Mode: Single Player vs. Multiplayer

In a single-player campaign, you are the only gamer on the playing field. This is the original and oldest mode for shooter games. If you play older games, you will find that many of them didn't even have a multiplayer mode. A gamer played through the campaign, posted up a high score, and that was it. It was time to trade in the game for a new one.

With the advent of multiplayer game modes, video game designers created a reason for gamers to hang onto those games.

Once the gamer had gotten familiar with the game in single-player mode, it was time to switch to multiplayer mode for capture-the-flag or Deathmatch games. A popular video game could have multiplayer servers available for years after the initial release of the game.

Single-Player Mode

When you first get an FPS game, you should play it in the single-player mode. This will allow you to get the hang of the game's mechanics before going online. When you first start playing, mess around a bit with things. Don't plan to move right in and complete the first level. If there's a practice mode, use that until you feel comfortable. If not, spend some time in the first level getting to know how the game works. This will serve you well in later missions.

The basic single-player mode is often called "Campaign Mode." In campaign mode, you will follow a storyline from beginning to end, like a book or a movie. As you complete each mission, you'll learn more of the story and be assigned a new mission that advances the storyline. Your missions will become increasingly more difficult until you complete your final mission – defeating a terrorist boss, saving a world leader, etc.

Playing all the way through the game in single-player mode can take some time and effort, but the experience you get in practicing your FPS skills as you do will make it much easier to play with other gamers in Multiplayer mode.

Multiplayer Mode

Playing in multiplayer mode is much different from playing in single-player mode. In single-player, you only have to worry about yourself. Even if you have a squad in your game, they are controlled by the game software, and you generally don't have to worry about them. In multiplayer mode, your squad is made up of other gamers that have as much at stake as you.

The classic multiplayer mode is a faceoff. Gamers compete directly against each other using the game's maps, internal mechanics, and weapons, but having no other relationship to the missions or campaigns in the single-player mode. In this type of multiplayer, the most common options are:

- Deathmatch – The classic player-versus-player free-for-all. In a Deathmatch game, the last gamer standing wins, so the simple rule is, "Don't Die." Many gamers don't like Deathmatch games because inexperienced players can hide out and let the other gamers kill each other off, only venturing from their hiding spots when one or two other players are left alive.

- Team Deathmatch – Team Deathmatch differs from Deathmatch in that players respawn after being killed. Team Deathmatch games are timed, and the goal is to record more kills than the other team(s) within the time limit.

- Capture the Flag - Players are split into teams that compete for control of the other team's flag. The flag can be literal or figurative. Some games require players to occupy a certain area of the opposing team's base in order to record a point, while other require players to snatch a flag or other object from the enemy base and return it to their own to record a point.

Although many new games still have these classic multiplayer modes, the current trend is Cooperative Story Mode. This mode is similar to single-player mode, in that players move through a storyline with corresponding missions of increasing difficulty. However, instead of just having one player, an entire squad of gamers linked through the internet are playing together to complete the mission.

Playing online is different from playing alone because you will need to interact with your squadmates. This is where having a headset with a good, noise-canceling microphone is a requirement. You and your squadmates will be talking tactics, reacting to what happens in the game, even discussing real-life plans. The experience of playing through an intense game is a bonding experience, and people who game together online often form tight-knit communities, even though they may never meet in real life.

Tournaments

As gaming has gotten more popular, video game tournaments have grown along with the communities. While the top tournaments require in-person attendance, open tournaments can be found online just by making a simple search.

Many gamers are drawn to online tournaments so they can test their skills against others. The excitement of competing in a tournament, moving through the competition brackets, is intense. There's nothing like the feeling of seeing yourself pitted against an experienced opponent and taking the win.

Gamers who compete in tournaments are an even more close-knit culture than those who game online. Tournament gamers all tend to know each other's strengths and weaknesses. They support other tournament gamers, helping them spot their flaws in order to make the group as a whole better. When you play in tournaments, you are often competing with people who have been gaming for decades. Don't get intimidated; instead, learn from your fellow tournament gamers.

There are a variety of different tournaments for diverse games available online. A gamer doesn't have to be limited to just one, Deathmatch-style tournament. Check the different tournaments that are available, and see what appeals to you.

Play Some of the Best First-Person Shooters

Over the years, game developers have produced some amazing games, and many forgettable ones. Rather than picking up the cheapest game or the one with the flashiest cover from your local games shop, check to see if any of these games are available for your system.

Halo 5

2015: Xbox One

In this fifth installment of the seminal *Halo* series, players once again step inside the armored suit of the human Spartan soldiers to fight against alien threats. The storyline revolves around Fire team Osiris, led by Spartan Locke, on a mission to track down the Master Chief and his missing Fire team Blue.

Unlike previous *Halo* games that supported up to four players on one console, this game is played solely over Microsoft's Xbox Live network, with each mission teaming four players on the network in cooperative story mode.

Call of Duty: Advanced Warfare

2014: Windows PC, PlayStation 4, PlayStation 3, Xbox One, Xbox 360

CoD:AW is a military sci-fi action shooter. The first *Call of Duty* game developed by Sledgehammer Games, it builds on the series by using a new game engine and adding a new feature, the "Exo," a personal exoskeleton, to boost the soldier's speed, jumping, and agility. *Advanced Warfare's* single-player storyline is considered the best in the franchise.

Titanfall

2014: Windows PC, Xbox One, Xbox 360

In *Titanfall*, gamers play as "pilots" to 20-foot battle exoskeletons called Titans. Pilots fight either on their own or from inside a Titan in battle. *Titanfall* has a multiplayer campaign mode and 5 head-to-head modes. The game has no single-player mode. The first solo game from the team behind the *Call of Duty* franchise, *Titanfall* won 60 awards at the 2014 E3 expo.

ZombiU
2012: Windows PC, WiiU, PlayStation 4, Xbox One

ZombiU puts a new twist on survival horror shooters. The player must survive in a zombie-infested London. Upon being bitten by a zombie, players switch to another human avatar, of which there are twelve. Any items collected by the player are held by the zombie-version of the character, which the player must now hunt down and kill to reclaim the inventory.

Half-Life 2
2004: Xbox, Xbox 360, PlayStation 3, Windows PC, Mac OSX, Linux, Android

In Half-Life 2, you play researcher Gordon Freeman, who must battle the aliens he accidentally unleashed on Earth in the original Half-Life. Half-Life 2 takes the suspense and the gut-wrenching charge of Half-Life and makes it more realistic, more intense, and more exciting to play. Half-Life 2 was the winner of 39 Game of the Year awards after its release, and has been referred to as the best game ever made.

ROLE-PLAYING GAME BASICS

An evolution of pen-and-paper role-playing games like Dungeons & Dragons, electronic role-playing games involve character creation and skill building through gaining experience points by completing missions. Many modern RPG's allow gamers to either complete a solo campaign mode or participate in cooperative missions.

One of the major draws of RPG's is character development. Gamers can choose to create player characters who look and act like themselves, or select a character who looks and acts completely unlike the gamer. A quiet, thoughtful person in real life may choose to be a brash, hack-and-slash character in the game. Someone who is unfailingly honest may choose to be a chaotic evil thief. There are so many options in RPG's, and at any time, the gamer's actions can change the character's alignment, skill sets, and inventory items.

One of the most popular forms of gaming today is the massively-multiplayer online role-playing game (MMORPG). This type of game is in turn an evolution of the text-based Multi-User Dungeons of the 1980's and 90's. The mechanics of these games allow hundreds of players to play in the same online world. Players can choose to complete missions on their own, team up, or battle against each other.

Most RPG's are presented in third-person mode, but some of the most popular MMORPG's use the first-person mode popular with FPS gamers.

Select an RPG

RPG's can be wonderful, exciting games. Selecting the right RPG, one that you'll really enjoy, can be difficult. Use these steps to select an RPG that you'll love playing.

1. What kind of game mechanics do you prefer? Combat in some RPG's is turn-based. You have the time to think about your attacks, selecting from your inventory of skills, before committing to a move. Others are

real-time – you need to know exactly which button presses will activate which skill in order to defeat your enemies.

2. MMO or solo RPG? If you don't have a lot of time to spend on your game, you'll want to buy a solo RPG game that will let you play only when you have the time. If you want to play with other players and you have the time to invest in it, look at an MMORPG.

3. What kind of world do you want to play in? RPG's come in several flavors. Many RPG's exist in fantasy worlds full of elves, trolls, dwarves, and humans. Others are set in sci-fi worlds with human and alien players. Some RPG's even let you play as a superhero or villain in a modern, urban setting.

4. How open do you want your RPG to be? Some RPG's are story and mission-based. At the completion of a mission, your total amount of experience is added up. At the close of the game, your decisions and experience gained will choose how the game ends. Others are open-

world, where your character can wander and take whatever path you choose. In an open-world RPG, you choose the missions you undertake, and can drop them or complete them at your leisure.

5. How complicated do you want your game to be? When you start playing RPG's, you'll want easy gameplay with a limited number of options. As you advance, you'll want the complexity of your games to become more advanced with you. Talk to other gamers and check reviews to find out if a game meets your complexity requirements.

Using these five steps will help you find RPG's that you'll surely enjoy playing.

Playing an MMORPG

MMORPG's have their own sets of rules, expectations, and game mechanics. The social aspect of these games is very important, and is unlike the social dimension in other game genres.

Joining a Guild

In most MMORPG's, you will team up with other players to form a guild. Most experienced players are already members of guilds, so you'll be looking for other beginning players who can play when you are available and are also looking to form a guild.

You can find these people in chat or in forums for your RPG. You should play with people you'll enjoy playing with. See what people are posting on the forums. Do they seem like interesting people to you? Engage them in conversation and see if their ideas about playing the game are similar to yours. When you find the right people, ask them to form a guild with you. If they are already in guilds, they may invite you to join theirs.

In many MMORPG's, balancing the abilities of your guild members is important. Having a guild made up all of warriors will make it hard to defeat many of your enemies. You'll need to look at how different abilities complement each other in order to know which characters you need to put together for a good playing group.

Etiquette in MMORPG's

There are some important rules of etiquette when it comes to MMORPG's. Knowing these rules will keep you from getting into trouble in MMORPG worlds.

Your character's name should be consistent with the world. When playing in a fantasy world, your character should have a fantasy name. An appropriate name for a dwarf warrior might be something like Throm Stormhammer. The same name wouldn't be appropriate for a sci-fi MMORPG. And there are very few games where naming your character after real-life people or items would be acceptable. If you go into a fantasy world with a name like iPod Jones, you may be reported to the game developers.

Unlike multiplayer FPS games, anything said in the open chat areas can be seen (or heard, if supported by your game) by everyone on that channel. Instead of talking about your car, school, job, etc., you are generally expected to stay in character unless you're in a private chat.

Many MMORPG's have rules about Out of Character (OOC) statements in chat. If players notice that you are consistently OOC, they can report you to the game's developers. If you don't listen to other player's reminders to stay in character or use abusive OOC language toward other players, the game developers can choose to suspend you from the game or ban you entirely.

Playing the Best RPG's

Role-Playing Games have been around for decades. Even though it's a very established genre, there are still games that stand out from the rest.

Diablo III

2012: Windows PC, Mac OSX, Xbox One, Xbox 360, PlayStation 4, PlayStation 3

Diablo III continues the storyline of the *Diablo* franchise. The protagonist is once again sent on a mission by the enigmatic scholar Deckard Caine, this time leading to a confrontation with Diablo's new human vessel as she leads the Lords of Hell in an assault on Heaven. Like *Diablo II*, *Diablo III* gives players access to Blizzard Entertainment's free Battle.net online multiplayer system, allowing gamers to participate in co-op battles or fight against each other in player vs. player mode.

Mass Effect 3

2012: Windows PC, Wii U, Xbox 360, PlayStation 3

The third and final installment in the *Mass Effect* series continues the saga of Commander Shepard. Shepard is on Earth when alien Reapers attack a colony world. The commander must discover the origin of the Reapers and how to defeat them for the last time. *Mass Effect 3* is unique among RPG series, in that importing a saved game from earlier in the series changes the way the game is played. In addition to a single-player story mode, the game also includes a four-player co-op mode.

Baldur's Gate: Enhanced Edition

2012: Windows PC, Mac OSX, Linux, Android, iOS

The original *Baldur's Gate*, released in 1998, was the first graphical RPG based on rules from Advanced

Dungeons & Dragons and based in the Forgotten Realms fantasy world. For the Enhanced Edition, the game and its add-on pack were rebuilt using the modern Infinity game engine. Not simply a remake, the Enhanced Edition adds several non-player characters and a multiplayer mode.

The Elder Scrolls 5: Skyrim
2011: Windows PC, Xbox 360, PlayStation 3

Skyrim is a story-based RPG based in a fantasy world. The main character must complete several missions leading to the defeat of the first dragon, Alduin, hailed and feared as a god of destruction. Rather than using a character-class system, *Skyrim* allows players to select different skills to learn and enhance over the course of the game.

World of Warcraft
2004: Windows PC, Mac OSX

The most popular MMORPG of all time, *World of Warcraft* (WoW) had 12 million subscribers at its height, and still has over 5 million today. *World of Warcraft* exists in an open fantasy world, where players receive missions in the form of "quests" suggested by non-player characters. The base game allows gamers to play on two lands from the original *Warcraft* games, Kalimdor and the Eastern Kingdoms. Expansion packs add new lands, characters, and quests for gamers to take on. *World of Warcraft* doesn't have an in-game guild system, instead allowing gamers to group up or go solo as they see fit.

STRATEGY GAME BASICS

While gamers who focus on tactics are playing first-person shooters, those who prefer the bigger picture are playing strategy games. Strategy games offer gamers the ability to plan a war from the perspective of a general. In a strategy game, the player has to balance resource availability, defensive planning, and offensive strength in order to win.

Strategy games trace their lineage all the way back through board games like Risk to the ancient strategy games of checkers and chess. Although not currently as popular a gaming genre as shooters and simulators, strategy games are still strong in the gaming ecosystem.

Strategy games present the player with an aerial view of the field. The area outside the player's immediate area is covered with the "fog of war," which must be scouted by units controlled by the gamer before the terrain will show up on the map. The player usually begins with a small number of workers, who can be put to work building training areas for troops and gathering resources. Workers generally have no attack capabilities, and are easily killed. It's best to train soldiers and send them scouting in order to discover more of the map.

All but a few strategy games are war games. Players engage in battles; train, move, and supply troops; conquer territories; and grind their enemies until they are utterly defeated. While many of these games are single-player campaigns against NPC opponents, the latest strategy games pit players against other players. This social aspect can make strategy gaming more fun, while also increasing the incentive to keep gaming.

Strategy games are divided into two basic categories:

Turn-Based Strategy (TBS)

TBS games are like graphical board games. Players gather resources, build, and make attacks on their own turns. Because the software can hold much more information than a physical board game, TBS games are infinitely more complex than board games, even though the mechanics of play are the same.

Real-Time Strategy (RTS)

RTS games require the gamer to think on the fly. Unlike TBS games, everything in the world is moving along at the same rate. Rather than watching other players' moves and calculating how to counteract them, RTS games are more realistic in that players never know what's coming until it happens. A gamer can send an orc army toward a human settlement, and the player controlling the humans won't know the army's on its way until it's spotted by the human scouts.

Although the two different categories of strategy games use very different gameplay mechanics, the basics of battle strategy games are the same.

Using the Tutorial

In the early days of gaming, every game was released with an instruction manual explaining how to play the game. This manual was easy to overlook, and many gamers simply set it aside in their zeal for getting right into the game. Today, with the "big box" game a thing of the past and so many games available as downloads, game developers program tutorials into their games rather than supplying instruction booklets.

Even if you've already played past games in a series, the tutorial will show you changes in units and gameplay from previous versions of the game. For first-time strategy gamers or gamers new to a game franchise, the tutorial is priceless. You won't need to blunder through your first couple of missions, hoping you're doing the right thing; the tutorial will teach you the skills you need to play the game.

Many strategy games begin with a tutorial level. This level takes you step-by-step through everything you need to know before having you play the actual game. Some of these games even ask if you want to play the tutorial or the campaign. While this method is effective, it still lets user skip the tutorial or forces them to sit through ten minutes of step-by-step instructions, no matter their skill level.

A tutorial method that is becoming more popular among developers is having a NPC assistant provide hints on what to do the first time you encounter the need for it. This way, players who have a lot of experience with strategy games can move right into playing without waiting through a tutorial, and those with less experience can listen to the hints and follow the assistant's instructions.

Playing a Campaign

The essential storyline of strategy gaming revolves around campaigns. Each battle won moves the player forward along the campaign, resulting in an ultimate victory, with the reward set by the campaign's storyline.

In most strategy games, each side represented in the war has its own campaign available. Players can play through each campaign as the commander of that side's forces. The ultimate outcome of one side's campaign may be completely different from the outcome of another side's.

Game developers often release expansion packs for strategy games that add new campaigns. Campaigns allow the game's designers to develop the strategy game with a certain look and feel, with specific units that can be deployed and the utilities to support them. Each new campaign comes with different maps, new and updated units, and new abilities.

Using Your Resources

Resource gathering and management is a key part of any strategy game. Know what resources you need and how to collect them. If your game uses berries as food, make sure that you place a resource-gathering building next to a good source of berries. If your game is currency-based, what is the source of the currency?

Resources in strategy games can either be renewable or non-renewable. In a game with non-renewable resources, you may have to fight an enemy for resource-rich territory. If you have renewable resources, you'll be more focused on keeping your enemy from destroying your resource collection and storage ability.

If your game uses workers to collect resources, make sure you have as many workers as your encampment will support. Often, the game will have a town hall that supports a certain number of workers. If a worker gets killed in an enemy attack, replace the worker as quickly as possible and put it back to work. Often, gamers run out of resources and lose a battle because their workers were killed when they weren't looking.

Almost all strategy games have resource storage buildings. There are usually two ways to get more resources: build more storage buildings, and upgrade your current storage buildings.

Keep track of how many resource buildings you are allowed to have and how far you can upgrade them. Try to keep your resource storage capacity topped out at all times. This will keep you from becoming strapped for available resources.

Resource management is the balance between collecting or generating resources and expending them on your units. If you only have enough resources to support the units you currently have, you could quickly lose your entire camp to an enemy attack. You should always make sure you have enough resources to have a troop reserve and train up new units to replace battle losses.

Balancing Defense and Offense

The balance of defense and offense is the second key in strategy gaming. In order to be successful, you have to expend your resources wisely to build up both.

Aggressive players often use the adage, "The best defense is a good offense." With this phrase, they try to justify building huge armies before placing a single defensive structure in their encampment. Sometimes, this strategy will work. If you can find and overwhelm your opponents early on in a battle, you can win with nothing but an army. This tactic often fails, however, because it can take some time to find the enemy's base. If the enemy has built defensive towers before your army arrives, the entire army can be destroyed before it can take out a single building.

The most experienced strategy gamers take a more balanced approach. More defense-minded players make building a defense tower an early priority, then begin training soldiers. Offense-minded players will begin by installing a training facility and starting troop training, then turn their attention to building a defensive facility. Whether defensive or aggressive, strategy gamers balance their time and resources in building and upgrading defensive structures and offensive units. Ignoring either one is a quick path to defeat.

Using a Hero Character

Many strategy games have Hero characters with special powers. Before taking the time and resources to get a Hero, find out exactly what the Hero does. Is it a skill or ability you're likely to use? Some Hero characters are geared toward a specific type of offensive strike, some are support units, and some are geared toward defense.

If a Hero character doesn't appeal to your style of play, then you're probably wasting resources to get that character. Instead, check to see what characters you might get with upgrades to your Hero facility. You might discover that the perfect Hero for you is just an upgrade or two away.

Hero characters can be very costly in resources and take a long time to train. It would be a shame to lose your Hero in the first few moments of an assault. Make sure that your Hero is always well supported by a good mix of other units. Even if your Hero character's ability is sneaking into facilities and unlocking doors, you'll want to provide your Hero with cover fire for escape once the task is done. Abandoning Hero characters to destruction can deplete your resources quickly.

Playing the Best Strategy Games

As one of the oldest video gaming genres, strategy gaming has a long list of amazing, innovative games, particularly for PC's. We'll list some of the best TBS and RTS games currently available here.

Plague, Inc. Evolved

2015: Windows PC, OSX, Linux, Xbox One

That rare strategy game that doesn't have you in command of an army, *Plague* instead has you in charge of a virus that has the ultimate goal of wiping out all of humanity. You have to evolve your virus to keep it ahead of the immune system and antivirals, but not let it kill so quickly that quarantines will be effective. The evolutionary balancing act makes this game deadly fun.

StarCraft II: Wings of Liberty

2010: Windows PC, Mac OSX

StarCraft II is a sci-fi real-time strategy game that continues the storyline of the original *StarCraft* game. With the alien Zerg threat pushed back, the human Dominion attempts to crush rebellion on its colony worlds. You are a member of the rebel forces, fighting back. On one colony world, you discover that the Zerg have returned, but the Dominion is ignoring them. It's up to the rebels to save humanity from the Zerg threat. *StarCraft II* has been praised for both its storyline and its gameplay, including a multiplayer cooperative feature that dynamically matches players of equal skill.

Civilization V
2010: Windows PC, Mac OSX, Linux

The fifth installment in the *Civilization* franchise, *Civ V* is a turn-based strategy game based on the idea of civilization building. Beginning in prehistoric times, players guide their civilization through to the far future. Players can win the game through research, exploration, diplomacy, military conquest, or several other conditions.

Halo Wars
2009: Xbox 360

Set in the *Halo* universe, this real-time strategy game pits humans against the alien Covenant for control of an ancient, highly advanced fleet of derelict alien spaceships. Although some experienced gamers have criticized the gameplay for feeling flat, the game received high praise for its detail and integration in the *Halo* franchise. To date, *Halo Wars* is the best-selling real-time strategy game on any console.

Command and Conquer: Red Alert 3
2008: Windows PC, Mac OSX, Xbox 360, PlayStation 3

The *Command and Conquer: Red Alert* series is a real-time strategy gamer based in an alternate reality where the Western Allies fought the Soviet Union in World War II. In *Red Alert 3*, the Soviets travel back in time, killing Albert Einstein, who played a large role in earlier installments of the series. This weakens the Western Allies, but unintentionally allows the rise of the Empire of the Rising Sun, creating a three-way war between Western, Eastern, and Soviet armies. Critics have praised the gameplay, particularly in multiplayer cooperative modes, along with the game's usability on gaming consoles.

SIMULATION GAME BASICS

Simulation games are games that imitate real-life activities. You can race cars, fly jets, even act out others' lives in simulation games. Vehicle simulation games are often incredibly realistic, replicating controls perfectly, while other simulation games might allow you to do things you could never do in real life.

Simulation games let the gamer practice learned skills and decision-making abilities while completing different goals in the game. Most simulation games are made for commercial sale by video game developers, but some, like the America's Army tactical simulation series released by the US Army, act as trainers or even recruitment tools.

Simulation games have great educational potential. Because many simulation games are similar to real-life interactions, they can teach players how to perform certain jobs or tasks. Simulation games can:

- Help players learn to manage resources for success.

- Show the cause-and-effect relationship between choices and the outcome of events.

- Display how actions effect the player's environment.

- Help players learn to respond appropriately to different situations.

- Teach players to accept responsibility for their actions.

- Give players an opportunity to try out different careers and professions.

There are three basic categories of simulation games:

Construction and Management Simulations (CMS)

These games allow players to build, expand, and/or manage fictional communities or projects with resources dictated by the game's mechanics. Unlike strategy games, where resource building is focused on attack and defense, CMS games are based on the principle that wise use of capital grows more capital. "Winning" in a CMS is accomplished by having a thriving project or community that has reached the highest level of advancement allowed by the game.

Sports and Professional Simulations

Sports and professional simulations allow gamers to step into the role of professional, athlete, or coach. While most of these simulations attempt to recreate their subjects with some realism, others satirize or fictionalize the represented activity. Flight simulators are often realistic down to the minutest detail, and major league athletics games are usually somewhat realistic, while racing games are often highly fictionalized.

Life Simulations

Life simulation games allow gamers to control the day-to-day lives of one or more characters. Life simulation games focus on building relationships and/or interacting with real or imagined ecosystems.

Choosing a Simulation Game

Because this is such a broad category, there are many options to choose from when selecting a simulation game. Here are some tips to keep in mind when looking for simulation games.

1. What scenario do you want to simulate? You could create cities, design theme parks, perform surgery, play football, go on a date, even mug an elderly woman.

2. Find a title that meets your need. Ask other gamers for recommendations of the best games for your interest. Search online to see what critics and reviewers have to say about different games.

3. Look at the gameplay. Do you prefer to do things in real time, as the game's world moves around you, or have time to think about your next step? Some simulations proceed step by step, others allow you to pause the action and make decisions, while others simulate real life by responding to the speed of your decision making.

4. Check the difficulty level. If you're looking at online reviews, you'll see that critics usually discuss how easy or difficult a simulation is to learn and manipulate. When you're just starting out, you'll want a simulation that is at a beginner to intermediate level.

5. Check system requirements. You may find the perfect game, only to discover that it requires more RAM than your PC has installed, that it requires accessory controllers that you don't have, or that it's only available for Xbox and you have a PlayStation. Don't buy a game before making sure it will work on your system.

Unlike shooters and RPG's, you don't usually have instant feedback about how well you're doing in simulation games. You may feel like the game is going well, only to get to a point where you can't continue because of decisions you've made earlier in the game. Don't let this discourage you; losing and restarting from scratch is an important part of learning to play simulation games. Being a good sport when you lose a simulation game is incredibly important, especially when playing online or with other players.

There are many single-task simulations available online, often for free. These simulators will give you a taste of what it's like to be in certain professions, such as being a surgeon or a truck driver. These are different from the educational game genre, in that they let you experience the situation rather than simply teaching you about a topic or testing you on your knowledge of that topic.

Playing the Best Simulation Games

With so many different games in the simulation category, it can be difficult to know what the best are. We'll list some of the best games in each category here.

X-Plane

1999-2016: Windows PC, Mac OSX, Linux, Android, iOS, WebOS

X-Plane is an accurate flight simulator that allows players to pilot commercial, military, and hobby aircraft from around the world in real and imaginary worlds. Its advanced physics engine sets it apart from other flight simulator games, because it allows users to create their own aircraft with simulated real-world performance. The game download includes World Creator, Aircraft Creator, and Airfoil Creator utilities, allowing users to create and share content with other players. *X-Plane* can be played in solo mode or a multiplayer online mode where players fly in the same world together. Its continuous development cycle means that gamers only have to purchase the game once to be eligible for lifetime upgrades.

The Sims

2000-2014: Windows PC, Mac OSX, Xbox 360, PlayStation 3, Wii, Nintendo 3DS.

The Sims is a series of games in which you control a character in a sandbox world described by the creator, Will Wright, as a virtual dollhouse. The console versions of the game introduced specific missions and goals based on the game's focus, while the PC-based versions focus instead on adding new abilities, items, and locations with each successive iteration and expansion pack for the game.

SimCity

1989-2013: Windows PC, Linux, Mac OS, Wii, Nintendo DS, iOS, Android

The granddaddy of urban planning simulators, the *SimCity* franchise allows users to play the role of City Manager in building a city from scratch. Based heavily on California development law and strategy, users zone areas for residential, commercial, and industrial use, build roads for cars and public transit, and provide basic utilities. As the city grows, users must adapt to the changing status of the city in order to help it become as prosperous as possible.

Madden NFL

1988-2016: Windows PC, Xbox One, Xbox 360, PlayStation 4, PlayStation 3

Madden NFL is the premier professional American Football simulator. The game allows players to lead real-life teams through multiple seasons and even create their own fantasy teams. Players select plays from team playbooks and control the player of their choice in completing the plays. EA Games, the developer of the franchise, releases a new *Madden NFL* game each year to reflect roster changes in the NFL teams. The last *Madden NFL* game released for Windows PC's was *Madden NFL '08*, with current development focused on the Xbox and PlayStation consoles.

Gran Turismo

1999-2016: PlayStation consoles

The *Gran Turismo* series of games puts the player in the driver's seat of a plethora of different racing and performance cars. Unlike some simulators that focus specifically on Formula 1 or NASCAR racing, *Gran Turismo* lets users race everything from stock cars to street sport vehicles like the Lamborghini Reventón on provided and player-generated tracks. *Gran Turismo* is the best-selling simulation game for the PlayStation family of consoles.

SOCIAL GAME BASICS

Social network gaming is a kind of gaming that is played on and integrated with social sites, particularly Facebook. Although there are many different genres of games available for play on social media sites, they share enough in common that they can be considered their own genre.

Social network gaming is the fastest growing gaming demographic. The games are wildly popular worldwide and have hundreds of millions of devoted players. From resource-building games to RPG's to combat games, there are social network games for every taste.

So, what makes social network gaming a unique genre? To begin with, virtually all social network games are free to play. Social network games make their money through advertising and through the purchase of in-game items. Some of the other things that make social network games unique are:

- Information regarding players' game standings are publicly available on the social network.

- The game world is independent from any individual players' game and play sessions.

- Game play events can be initiated by specific real-time events occurring.

- The rules of a game instance can change as game play takes place.

- Players are encouraged to return frequently to a certain part of the game space.

- Tasks considered "easy" need to be repeated frequently.

- Games are designed to support players entering and leaving ongoing game sessions.

- Some parts of the game space are private to a single player.

- Games make use of other players' game instances to provide input to the overall game state.

- The game can change or rearrange game elements to form elements that are more complex.

- Game resources may be managed for their own sake.

- Players may be granted temporary access to other players' private game spaces.

- The game supports actions that only have explicit benefits for somebody other than the one who is performing the action

- Players can receive help in games by actions from social networking friends who are not playing the game.

- Inviting new players to the game is a game action that results in a reward.

- Game events are broadcast on the social network where others can view them.

- Compound actions require several players to perform actions.

- Players perform actions to help others under the assumption that they later will be helped in return.

- Gamers try to influence other players' actions based upon moral grounds.

- Some actions within a game have pre-defined effects on the social network outside the game system.

While this entire list doesn't apply to every social network game, every social network game has some of the elements listed here.

If you are a member of a social network, you've probably received an invitation to join a social network game. If you would like to start playing social network games, accepting one of those requests would be a good place to start.

Facebook is adept at matching advertising to your personal interests. In addition to accepting requests, check the game ads that Facebook runs on your feed. If you have noted an interest in strategy war games, you may find that Facebook is already showing you a social network strategy game that you could join.

If you don't have friends who are already social gamers and haven't seen anything advertised in your social network's feed, you can search to see what games in your preferred genre are supported by your social networking site. Check reviews on the games you are looking into, and be wary: some social network game developers will happily sell the information they glean from your social network profile to third parties.

How to be a Top Social Network Gamer

Unlike other gaming genres, no one wins in a social network game. The games are designed to allow an infinite progression. How good you are in the game is based on how your stats compare to your friends' stats, and in the wider world of the game, how they compare to the stats of every other player.

To get top stats in a social network game, you have to play as often as possible. Since the game world is constant, the longer you are in it, the more points you can rack up. This is true in virtually every social network. Many games even reward you for being online by protecting you from raids by other players as long as you remain active.

Be willing to spend a bit of money for upgrades and advantages. Although social network games on the whole are free to play, you can usually trade real money for in-game credits that you can use to upgrade equipment, buy weapons, etc. If you're independently wealthy and can afford to buy every upgrade instantly, feel free. For everyone else, you will need to balance your upgrade times with whatever you can afford to spend on speeding things up. One good strategy is to buy upgrades that you need to make a plan work while you're online, then set any other time-intensive upgrades you want into motion before you go offline.

And finally, social network games often contain in-built gifting systems, where other players can give you things you need if you ask for them. Be friendly! The more social you are, the more likely people will be to give you the things you need!

Playing the Best Social Network Games

The problem with social network games is that they are constantly changing. Unlike games that you can buy once and play forever, social network games go online, and are retired when the developers aren't making enough money off of them. Some of the most popular social network games lost popularity quickly when new games came out and supplanted them. On Facebook, some of the most popular games have included FarmVille, Hero Academy, CityVille, MafiaWars, The Sims Social, and Empires & Allies. Many of these top games have been retired or switched to mobile platforms since their release, and may not be available to play.

GAMING CHEAT AND HACK BASICS

In the early days of video games, developers would hide ways to circumvent certain game limitations for testing purposes. Even in text-based adventure games, entering certain passcodes would allow testers to skip to newly coded areas of the game for testing. Eventually, game developers started adding "cheat codes" as Easter Eggs for gamers to discover.

One of the most famous console cheat codes is the "Konami Code" for the Nintendo Entertainment System. The sequence of button presses was the result of a developer needing an easier way to play through a difficult game to test his coding. The code gave a full set of all power-ups to the player. When the programmer, Kazuhisa Hashimoto, realized he'd left it in the code after the game had already launched, he came up with the idea to add it as an Easter Egg in subsequent games.

On the PC, the cheat codes award goes to DOOM, the seminal 1993 shooter by id Software. The game was so complicated to design that the developers created a cheat code system, prefixing their code words with the letters "id." By release time, the developers had had so much fun with all of the different cheats that they decided to leave them in and wait for gamers to discover them.

The best place to find cheat codes is in forums about your game. Simply go to any web browser and do a search for "cheat codes for [game]." You may have to join the forum before you can see what's posted there, but creating gaming forum memberships is always a good idea.

While cheats may be great fun when you're playing alone, modifying your game in online or multiplayer games looked at as cheating. Many games won't allow you to use cheat codes in multiplayer modes or kick you offline if you use cheat codes while in online mode.

Hacking games, on the other hand, is always considered cheating. In the days of cartridge-fed consoles, add-on devices such as the Game Shark for the Sega Master System and the Game Genie for the NES artificially tricked games into adding lives, weapons, or points to your score. You could use these devices to skip between levels, and do just about anything you wanted. Having one of these devices often resulted in the owner being shunned by other gamers.

While today's consoles aren't as vulnerable to hacks as the second-generation consoles, today's PC games face their own code-altering challenges. Hackers look for exploits that they can run against the software they buy, writing pieces of code they can run against the games software to change the way the game works. Although this isn't illegal, it does become a problem when a gamer uses a hacked game in an online, multiplayer setting.

Using hacked games on an online service can be grounds for being expelled from the server and having your account deleted. In addition, the service provider may contact to the authorities to report your hacked software for possible piracy, since most people don't hack their own software but download hacked software from pirate sites.

Rather than angering other players and risking account loss, fines, and even jail time, it's best simply to play it straight when you're gaming online.

GAMING FINANCE BASICS

When you're a new gamer, it can be easy to get into financial trouble. From overextending yourself in buying the latest games and accessories to having your financial information stolen while buying games online, you need to keep your money safe and under your control.

BUDGETING BASICS

Before you can decide how much you can spend on gaming, you need to know how much money you have available to make gaming purchases. Don't fall into the habit of gamblers, spending all your money on games, then begging money off of friends and relatives in order to survive long enough to buy the next game. You need to start your gaming adventure with an understanding of how to budget your money.

Keep Track of Where Your Money is Going Now

Take a month and write down everywhere you spend your money, whenever you spend money. This will give you an idea of where your money is going now.

Mark down all of your monthly bills. Look at your phone, utilities, internet service, rent or mortgage, student loans, any consumer debt you're paying down, and contributions to your savings or retirement accounts. Monthly bills are your top priority.

Next, look at how much money you're spending on food, clothing, and travel expenses. These are your second-priority, necessary expenses.

Finally, look at what you spend on entertainment, going out with friends, drinking, etc. These are discretionary expenses. This is money that you could be using on gaming.

Use the Envelope System

In the classic envelope system, you put enough cash into one envelope to pay all of your monthly bills, enough in a second to pay your necessary expenses, and the rest in a third envelope for your discretionary expenses.

If you're like most people these days, your bills are almost all paid online. Another way to use the envelope system is to use three separate bank accounts. Set up one account for your monthly expenses, one for your necessary expenses, and one for discretionary expenses.

If you have an account that your bank direct deposits funds to, set up automatic transactions on that account with your bank to move the right amounts of money to the other accounts. Then use the right accounts for each expense or purchase.

Review your Accounts Regularly

Keep an eye on what you're spending and what's in your accounts. If you start spending less money on monthly expenses or necessary expenses, the excess will build up in your accounts. Transfer that extra into a savings account and redo your automatic account transfers to move more money in the future to your discretionary account.

FIND WAYS TO SAVE

Once you start keeping track of your money, you can begin finding ways to save money on expenses you don't want and redirect them to gaming.

Start saving by living a healthier lifestyle. If you smoke, do what you can to quit. The average smoker today spends over $1,000 each year on cigarettes. Not only will you be healthier and less likely to die of cancer, but with that money, you could buy one brand new game every three weeks. If you drink, limit your alcohol intake.

Think about how often you eat out. If you regularly eat at restaurants, try eating in more often. If you still feel like you need to eat out, choose less expensive options in items or restaurants. It may amaze you how fast eating out adds up.

Comparison shop and price match. Rather than buying what you want, when you want it, see if you can find a better price. There's no reason not to stop in the middle of a store and search your favorite online sites to see if the price online is better. When shopping for groceries or other products, check to see if your store has a price-matching app. This can save you several dollars on each shopping trip. Before you buy fuel for your vehicle, check prices online. You can use Google Maps' gas station price feature to make sure you're getting the best price without driving too far out of your way.

KEEP YOUR FINANCIAL INFORMATION SAFE

No matter how careful you are with your money, if someone gets your financial information, you could lose everything.

Here are some tips for keeping your financial information safe when buying games and accessories or signing up for online services.

- Make it a habit to read the website's security and privacy policy. Before you give your financial information to any website, check the website's security policy. You need to know how the website plans to keep your information safe. In addition, the privacy policy will tell you if the website shares any of your information with third parties.

- Check if they use SSL security. If you are one of those people who love to download online games or even buy products on the internet, the principal thing that you have to consider is whether the site that you are using has secure connections. You'll know they are secure if they have https at the beginning of the web address instead of just http. If you see that they don't have an official SSL certificate then don't buy their merchandise or services online.

- Never share your password with others. Make sure that others can't get into your account. If you think your account may have been hacked, change your password immediately.

- Do not put any important information on online social networking sites. Even if your account is limited to friends, someone could see your information and jot it down.

- Don't put your birthplace or birth year in your online accounts. Identity thieves can use this kind of information to apply for credit cards in your name.

- Install an anti-virus program on your PC. It's important to protect your PC from programs that try to steal your financial information.

- Don't download or install browser extensions. Search helpers and add-ons can hide malicious programs that keep track of your keypresses looking for combinations that could be credit card numbers and birth dates.

GAMING HEALTH BASICS

In the past, gaming has been blamed for health problems like vision loss, reduced mental capacity, and aggression. Research has found that there is no correlation between these problems and playing video games.

Health problems related to gaming can be symptomatic of gaming addiction. Gaming addiction is characterized by an uncontrollable desire to play video games. Gamers become addicted to games for many reasons. If you think that you or someone you know might be a gaming addict, you should seek professional help.

Some of the health symptoms and effects of gaming addiction include:

• Sleep Deprivation

With school and/or work eating so much of modern people's time, many people sacrifice their sleeping hours to game instead. Gaming addiction and extended periods without sleep may result in a sleeping disorder, with the attendant ill health effects.

• Seclusion and Isolation

An excessive amount of gaming can lead people to seclude themselves from family and friends. Communicating with squadmates through the game may take priority over interacting with family and friends in the real world. The combined effects of sleep deprivation and seclusion can result in a sickly appearance.

• Ignoring Personal Hygiene

When people become addicted to video games, one of the most obvious early signs is a lack of personal hygiene and cleanliness. With little interaction in the real world, gamers may feel that they don't need to care for themselves.

• Stress and Depression

Stress caused by gaming addiction can be caused by frustration with the video game itself, or with real life problems caused by the addiction. Addicted gamers may find themselves out of money, out of friends, and on the bad side of family members. This leads the gamer to retreat even further into the game, which increases the stress even more and leads to a depressive cycle.

• Carpal Tunnel Syndrome and Arthritis

Too much game playing may result in some physical weakness, for example, joint inflammation (arthritis) and carpal tunnel syndrome. Studies have suggested that long hours playing on video game controller can cause gradual damage to finger joints. Carpal tunnel syndrome is caused by the collapse of the carpal tunnel in the wrist on the carpal nerve. It causes nerve pain and limited hand movement. This is particularly an issue in PC gaming addicts.

• Unhealthy Diet

To support their addiction, gaming addicts will pick prepared dinners and fast food over more nutritional diets. Gamers also use caffeinated drinks and sugary sodas to keep them going during late-night binge playing. Such habits may result in diabetes, obesity, and other health conditions.

• Idle Lifestyle

Addicts who spend most of their available hours gaming are not likely to be getting enough exercise. Resting or sitting throughout the day while playing games, combined with poor eating habits and lack of sleep, is a dangerous combination that may result in heart disease, hypertension and strokes.

• Violent Behavior

Although gaming in itself doesn't cause violent behavior, gaming addicts often react violently when they are interrupted in their gaming or taken away from their games. This is caused by the stress and anxiety involved in the gaming addiction, and also because the gamer feels safe while playing the game, and the person interrupting the game is violating that safety.

• Denial

Lying and denial to disguise unusual behavior is among the fundamental signs that video gaming is becoming an addiction. Addicts will justify and blame others for the obvious issues of their gaming addiction. As the addiction continues to worsen, the gaming addict continues to believe the there is no problem.

Gaming can be a fun, positive pastime that brings you years of enjoyment. It can expand your social circle and give you new and useful skill sets. However, if you aren't careful with your time and money, it can become an addiction that damages your health and your relationships.

CONCLUSION

Love it or hate it, gaming is here to stay. Today's games are available in a variety of genres—from strategy to role playing. Because games are available in nearly every "flavor" under the sun, there is potentially a game out there that every person will enjoy. This enjoyment, however, is not without risks. The biggest risks to games are financial and health-related. That's why it's important to set a budget when buying games for a personal console or playing them online, or you could find yourself in poverty. No matter how interactive or immersive the virtual world you are in, it's also important to take breaks and interact with reality often, as humans weren't made to sit in front of a screen all day. Another risk is video game addiction. Knowing the basics about gaming will help us avoid pitfalls in the future as video games evolve and become a more integral part of our lives in modern society.

ABOUT THE AUTHOR

Corey Hardin is an avid gamer. His favorite game series include Fallout (of course) Halo, Resident Evil and Bioshock. He wants to earn enough money to buy his own private island, so that he can escape the coming Zombpocalypse.

Other books by Corey Hardin

Vault Dweller's Secrets: An Unofficial Guide to Fallout 4